# DING DONG BAZAAR

**STREET**
**GRAPHICS**
**EGYPT**

**AIR CONDITIONED**

# STREET GRA

with over 150 colour illustrations

Thames & Hudson

**For my daughter, Nicky**

Info: streetgraphics@fsmail.co.uk

**Thanks to:**
Giza: Mohammed Saad Auad
Cairo: 'Dr Ragab's Pharaonic Village' and 'Magic Land'
Khan el-Khalili: Moustafa Abd El Fattah
All the street vendors of Cairo, Luxor, Aswan, Hurghada and
    Alexandria who permitted photography
New York: Paula Gilhooley and Eileen Connor

**Sources:**
E. A. Wallis Budge, *Egyptian Magic*, New York, 1971
Aidan Dodson, *The Hieroglyphs of Ancient Egypt*, London, 2001
*The Egyptian Book of the Dead*, trans. E. A. Wallis Budge,
    New York, 1967 (1st ed. 1895)
Ian McMahan, *Secrets of the Pharaohs*, New York, 1998
Anthony S. Mercatante, *Who's Who in Egyptian Mythology*,
    Lanham, MD, 1995
Catharine Roehrig, *Fun with Hieroglyphs*, New York, 1990
Anthony Sattin, *The Pharaoh's Shadow*, London, 2000
Richard H. Wilkinson, *Symbol and Magic in Egyptian Art*,
    London, 1994

First published in the United Kingdom in 2003 by
Thames & Hudson Ltd, 181A High Holborn, London WC1V 7QX

www.thamesandhudson.com

© 2003 Thames & Hudson Ltd

British Library Cataloguing-in-Publication Data
A catalogue record for this book is available from the British Library

ISBN 0-500-28433-4

Printed in Hong Kong by H&Y Printing Ltd

# CONTENTS

# INTRODUCTION

## 'Man fears time but time fears the pyramids.'

**Egyptian proverb**

Street graphics – the signs, symbols and imagery of urban life – are not a recent phenomenon. The streets of ancient Egypt featured religious and state propaganda carved on a monumental scale as early as 3000 BC. The ancient Egyptians developed their written language of hieroglyphs with a concern for its aesthetics and flexibility: multidirectional symbols that could be grouped together in different ways meant greater creative possibilities for adorning the challenging forms of pharaonic temples, tombs and monuments.

Inanimate objects, insects, animals, birds, humans and gods were rendered as graphic symbols to convey both concepts and phonetic sounds: the image was the message. The same hieroglyphs were used to refer both to the concepts of drawing and writing and their venerated practitioners, the scribes: a palette, water pot and reed pen represented both art and artist. Masons carved the scribes' work into stone that has survived both the demise of the culture it depicts, two millennia ago, and the centuries of wanton destruction that followed.

**Opposite** Present-day reality for the sole remaining Wonder of the World is not the isolated desert setting so often portrayed in books. The pyramids stand on the edge of urban Giza, shrouded in the pollution of nearby Cairo. Amid the masses of guides, souvenir hawkers and the clashing holiday outfits of international tour groups, they remain awesome.

## 'There is no darkness like ignorance'
**Egyptian proverb**

Subsequent Greek, Roman, Christian and Muslim periods of Egyptian history saw hieroglyphic imagery transform from communication into conundrum, intriguing visitors from Herodotus in the 5th century BC onwards. The language, faith and culture that the hieroglyphs described were no longer understood and became subject to speculative interpretation. Napoleon's 1798 invasion of Egypt provided the breakthrough, starting an unabated international fascination with the imagery of the pharoahs. A monumental slab of stone discovered by French troops in 1799, with inscriptions in three languages –

Egyptian hieroglyphs, demotic script and Greek – had addressed the cosmopolitan citizens of an Egyptian city in 196 BC. Named the Rosetta Stone, it became the key to hieroglyphic decipherment and modern understanding of ancient Egyptian culture.

Egypt's antiquities were catalogued during the French occupation and *Description de l'Egypte*, published in the early 19th century, described an exotic culture that captured Western imaginations. Egyptology became a science, orientalism became a fashion, and Thomas Cook used Egypt's popularity to launch a new industry, tourism.

**Opposite** A detail from the facade of Alexandria's new library, opened in November 2002, featuring carved letterforms from the world's alphabets. Alexandria's ancient library was founded by Ptolemy I, the Greek ruler of Egypt from 305 to 282 BC; its legendary collection grew until the building was destroyed by fire during the reign of Cleopatra (51–30 BC).

# 'Egypt is an image of the heavens, and the whole cosmos dwells in this sanctuary.'

**Luxor temple inscription**

Modern-day Egypt generates major revenue from tourism, and the visual and imaginative appeal of the ancient world remains powerful. Representations both predictable and unpredictable assail visitors: you can stay at the Ramses Hotel, ride a camel called Tutankhamun or meet Cleopatra at a popular Cairo theme park. Souvenir stalls sag under the theme of pharaonic Egypt. Reproductions and questionable interpretations abound – a scarab T-shirt for the budget backpacker or a golden sphinx in a crystal pyramid sandstorm of glinting gold dust for the creditcard-toting tourist.

Beyond the imagery of tourism, contemporary Egyptian street graphics are rendered in the calligraphic script common to all Islamic cultures. Western-style advertising imagery is growing in popularity, but remains distinctively Egyptian across the fields of catering, entertainment, signs and services. This collection of images is a subjective glimpse at Egypt's street graphics in 2002.

**Opposite** Bottles of perfume, posters and hieroglyphic henna 'tattoos' on offer outside a tourist store in Hurghada.

# HIEROGLYPHS

'Bring me a water-pot and palette from the writing-kit of Thoth and the mysteries which are in them.'

*The Egyptian Book of the Dead*

**Opposite** Temple detail featuring three *ankh* symbols. The *ankh* signified life and therefore power; it is often depicted in the hands of figures representing gods or pharaohs who have been granted divine status.

**Above** An oval cartouche signified the pharaoh's kingdom and contained hieroglyphs representing royal names.
**Right** A temple detail featuring the pyramidion and *ankh* symbols. The latter passed into Christian symbolism through Egypt's Coptic Church and more recently, has entered modern rock music iconography.

**Above left** Early hieroglyphs were pictorial signs that originally represented the object they referred to. These then developed into symbols representing the phonetic sounds of language. The owl no longer meant a bird but the consonant 'm', depicted here along with the 'sycamore tree' and 'beer jug' symbols, as letters in a temple wall inscription.

**Above centre** A restored panel features the sacred Tet pillar of Osiris (representing the double consonant 'dd') combined with the *ankh*, a symbol of life, to signify the supreme divinity of Osiris.

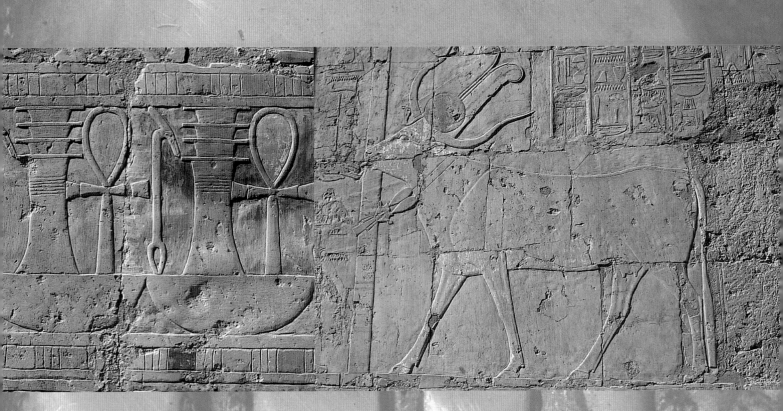

**Above right** Apis, the sacred bull of Memphis, the capital of ancient Egypt, is depicted carrying the sun between his horns and accompanied by hieroglyphic text. Originally fertility symbols, bulls became revered as divine and were accorded embalming and burial rites similar to those of the pharaohs.

**Overleaf** Entrance tickets to four of Egypt's principal historic sites, which include hieroglyphs in their design. The second ticket permits entry to the temple of Hatshepsut (background), situated below towering cliffs on the Nile's west bank in Luxor, site of the ancient city of Thebes.

At the entrance to each of Egypt's historic sites, visitors run the gauntlet of street vendors pushing their wares, including ceramic and resin reproductions of ancient Egyptian art.

**Overleaf** Hieroglyphs are popular with tourists: they are painted on hotel walls, printed on T-shirts and used to fill postcard racks outside souvenir stores. Left, a postcard depicts the eye of the falcon-headed god Horus, a protective symbol. Right, the scarab is a sacred dung beetle, signifying the god Kheper who copulated with his own shadow. The sun symbol between its legs represents the beetle's dung ball and its continuous rolling signifies the daily movement of the sun.

متحف التحنيط

# SIGNS & SYMBOLS

'It is better not to know and know that you do not know than to presumptuously attribute some random meaning to symbols.'

**Luxor temple inscription**

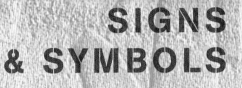

**Opposite** A sign depicting an ancient Egyptian embalming room advertises 'Dr Ragab's Pharaonic Village'. This Cairo theme park ushers visitors through tableaux populated by actors in ancient Egyptian dress.

Anonymous-looking metal boxes litter the streets of Egyptian cities. The skull and crossbones symbol indicates that they should be left alone.

**Below** Hand-painted advertising for a brand of batteries equates product longevity with the nine lives of a cat.
**Opposite** A cut-out policeman, universally ignored by motorists in Alexandria.

Road markings in the Mediterranean city founded by Alexander the Great depict one of the seven wonders of the ancient world: the Pharos commissioned by Ptolemy I. Until its destruction in the early 14th century, the lighthouse marked a safe sea route to Alexandria and remains a potent symbol of the city's history.

Road and telephone signs in Aswan, a subway sign in Alexandria and a street sign in Luxor.
**Overleaf** Advertising sign for 'Sindbad Submarine' in the Red Sea coastal town of Hurghada.
Glass-bottomed boats are a popular way of seeing Egypt's rich marine life without getting wet.

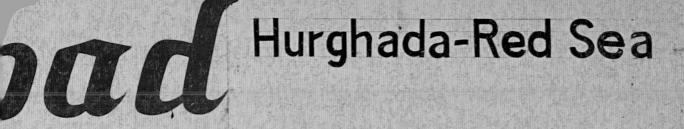

*bad* Hurghada-Red Sea

*ine*

l. 442166-443261/6 Fax.443267

Parking inwrongPlaces
Will Makeyou
accountableto Law
Apartfrom being
atresPassingontheRight
oftheCitizenandthestate

# LUXOR TEMPLE

**OPEN:**

**SUMMER**
FROM 6 AM TO 10 PM

**WINTER**
FROM 6 AM TO 9 PM

**TICKETS:**

| | | |
|---|---|---|
| FOREIGNER | L.E | 20 |
| F. STUDENT | L.E | 10 |
| TRIPOD | L.E | 20 |

HOUSE OF OSIRIS

FREE OF HASSLE SHOP

**Opposite** A sign in the historic city of Luxor states 'Parking in wrong places will make you accountable to law apart from being a trespassing on the right of the citizen and the state'.

**Above left** Admissions signs to temples in Luxor may appear rather impolite, identifying visitors as foreigners, but photographers, presumed foreign and possibly wealthy, face an even heavier entry price.

**Above right** Luxor has more 'No hassle' signs than other Egyptian cities and rightly so.

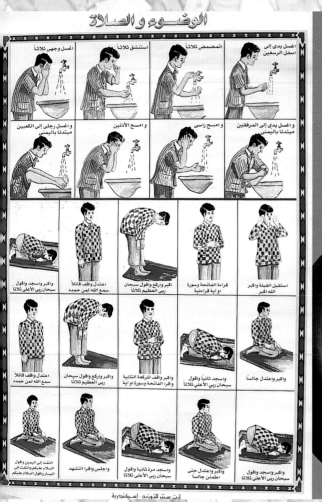

صور
٦ × ٤
فـي
الحـال

PASSPORT PHOTOS

**Left** A street vendor's poster shows children the way to wash and to pray according to the Koran.
**Centre** An optician's sign in Alexandria. **Right** A sign advertising passport photos in Giza.

H O BAKSHISH O

# T-SHIRTS

### 'Little is better than nothing.'
**Egyptian proverb**

**Opposite** A T-shirt design representing two memorable aspects of visiting Egypt: the popular *galabiya* robe, and *bakshish*, a payment demanded for small services that are frequently not requested and often not received.

T-shirt vendors speak at length about the quality of renowned Egyptian cotton but say little about T-shirt designs. Egypt is 95 per cent desert and camels are a popular representation of the Egyptian experience.

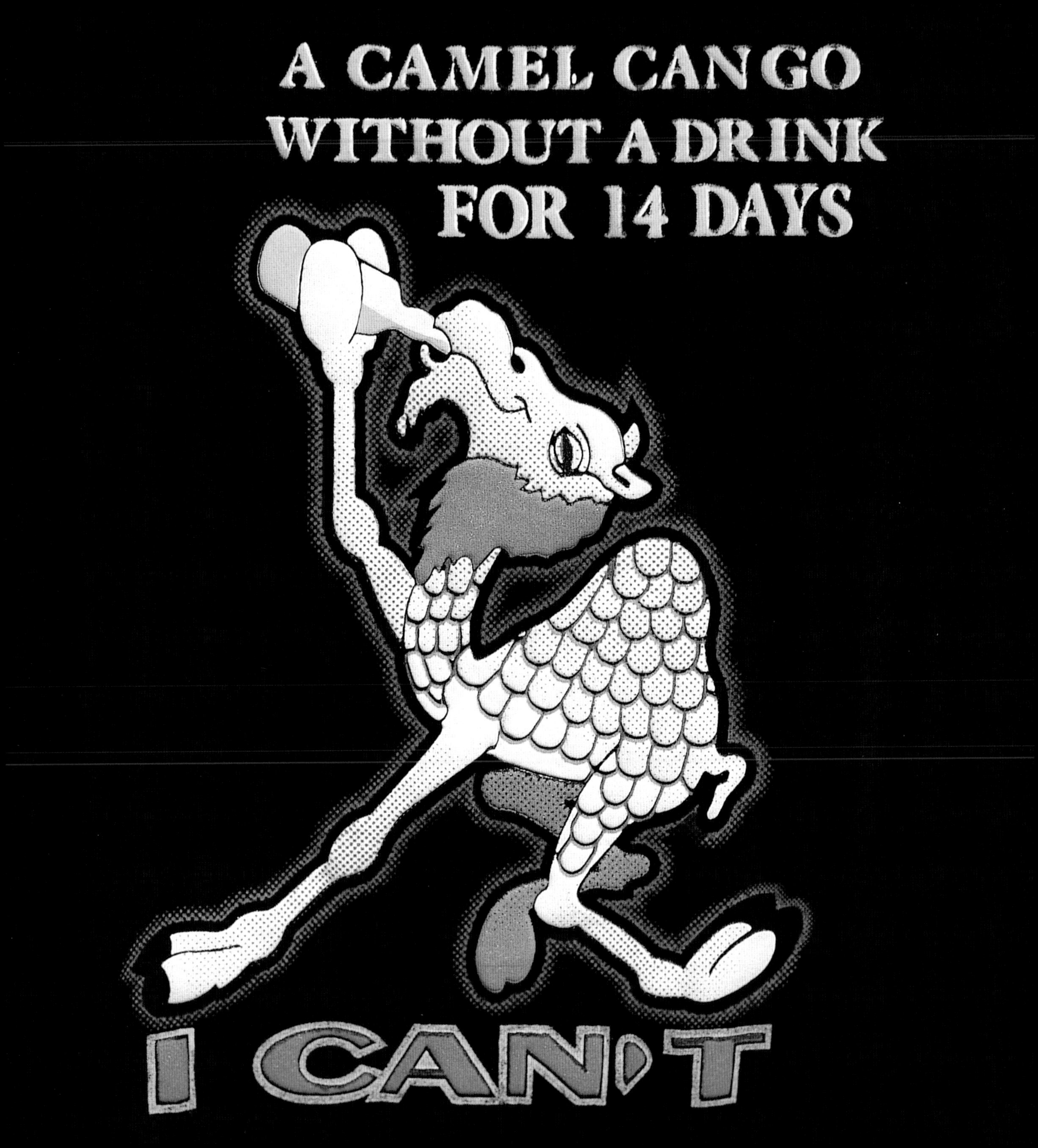
A CAMEL CAN GO
WITHOUT A DRINK
FOR 14 DAYS
I CAN'T

In addition to the historic sites and the deserts represented by the ubiquitous camel, tourists also come to dive at the Red Sea resorts of Hurghada, Sharm el-Sheikh and Dahab. The sea adds different image possibilities to the usual range of T-shirt designs and slogans.

**Overleaf** For female visitors to Egypt's Red Sea resorts who may receive unwanted attention, a T-shirt offers a less than subtle cultural reminder.

DON'T

THE

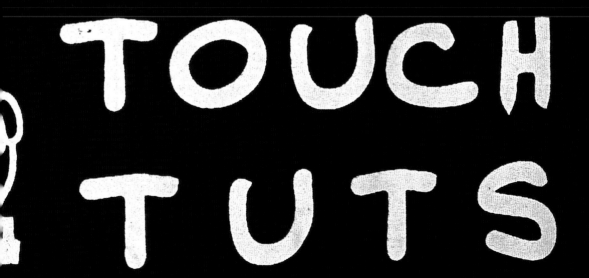

TOUCH
TUTS

T-shirts in Cairo's Khan el-Khalili souk cover all that Egypt has to offer, including mythical surfing pharaohs.

# WALL PAINTINGS

'Images are closer to reality
than cold definitions.'

**Luxor temple inscription**

**Opposite** Entering the Nubian city of Aswan, a mural depicts
Egyptian president Hosny Mubarak with the national flag
and Aswan's principal attractions: the ancient temple of
Philae, and Felucca sailing boats on the Nile.

49

Where wall paintings and murals are found, the tried and tested imagery of the pharaohs remains the most popular. If you don't have time to visit Upper Egypt's temple of Abu Simbel you can see it represented on the wall of Dr Fox's alabaster factory in Luxor or the Abu Simbel café in Aswan's souk.
**Overleaf** Murals on a store selling alabaster souvenirs.

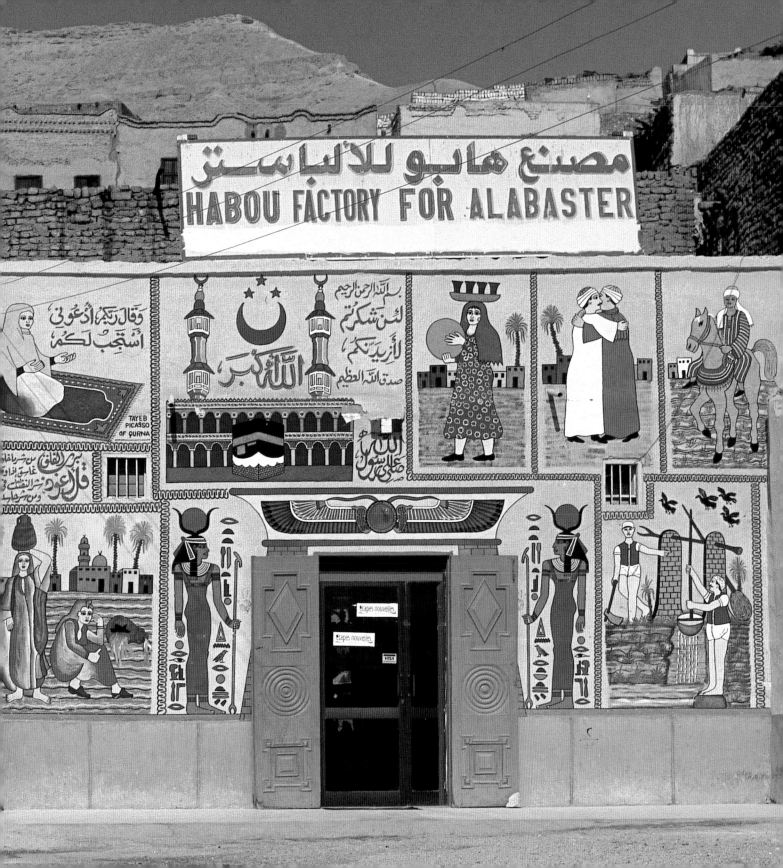

Near Luxor, on the west bank of the Nile, is Qurna, a collection of villages that covered the site of ancient Egypt's royal burial site, the Valley of the Kings, and was home to many of the original 'tomb raiders'. Qurna's wall paintings of traditional village life compete with the pharaonic imagery that draws tourists to its alabaster shops.

**Previous pages** A Qurna wall painting shows a youth watching women bake bread.
**Below** A village man leading his camel.

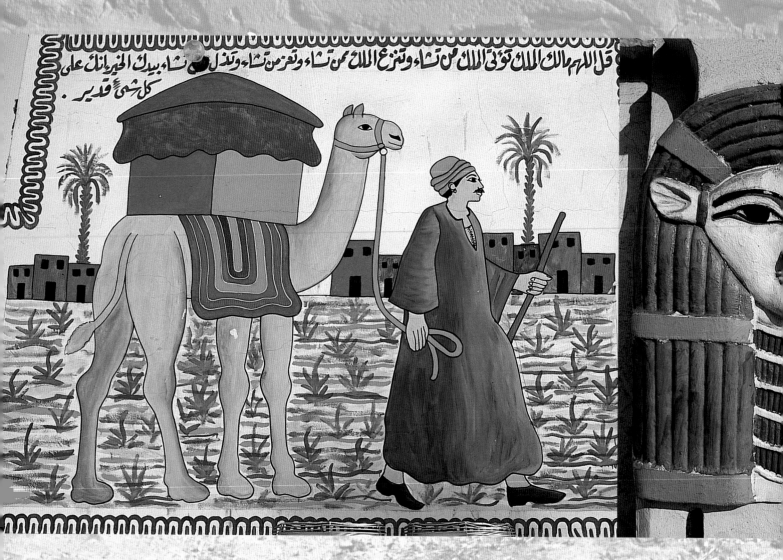

Below centre Portrait of the goddess Hathor, 'Dr Ragab's Pharaonic Village' theme park, Cairo.
Below right Village women cope with broken pots and the daily chore of hauling water.

وَأْمَا بِنِعْمَةِ رَبِّكَ فَحَدِّث

Overleaf Traditional imagery in Qurna emphasizes the work of village women, with men depicted as onlookers or passers-by.

**Above** A mixture of traditional, ancient and modern wall paintings.

Below Crumbling buildings of old Qurna with their fading wall paintings.

Slunečny
wyz. Veladni
d Leta 1741

4 73

Pamat: Nebefy

1664 5o 65.

315

712

# BOOK COVERS

**'If thou wouldst read a book possessed of magical powers, come with me and I will show it to thee.'**

*The Tale of Setne*, Ptolemaic period papyrus

**Opposite** Sculpted books and mosaics at the gates of Alexandria's university remind students of the city's academic legacy as a classical seat of learning.

In Islam the djinn is an evil spirit that tempts believers from righteous ways. On the streets of Egyptian cities are displays of books with lurid covers which highlight the dangers of djinn temptation and how to deal with them.

زواج الجان من بنى الإنسان

محمد عبده مغاورى

كيفية زواج الجان من بنى الإنسان

تأليف
أبو محمد جمال بن محمد الشامى

عبد الله نواره

مكتبة الايمان بالمنصورة
أمام جامعة الأزهر
ت ٢٥٧٨٨٢

**Opposite** Detail from the cover of a 'guidebook' to the first night of marriage.

**Below** Books explaining the evils of prostitution have covers depicting women with censored eyes.

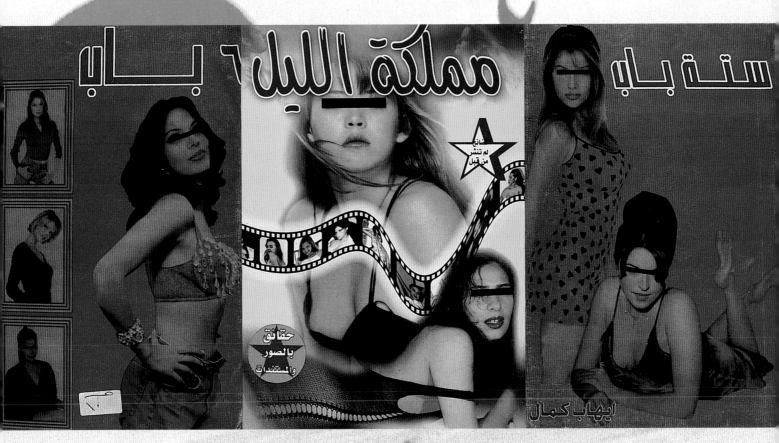

**Overleaf**

**Page 72** Book cover details, from left to right: a book on palmistry, a book about headaches both great and small, a face screaming in agony, and finally an Arabic translation of Adolf Hitler's *Mein Kampf*.

**Page 73** Cover detail of a book entitled *The Evil Eye*.

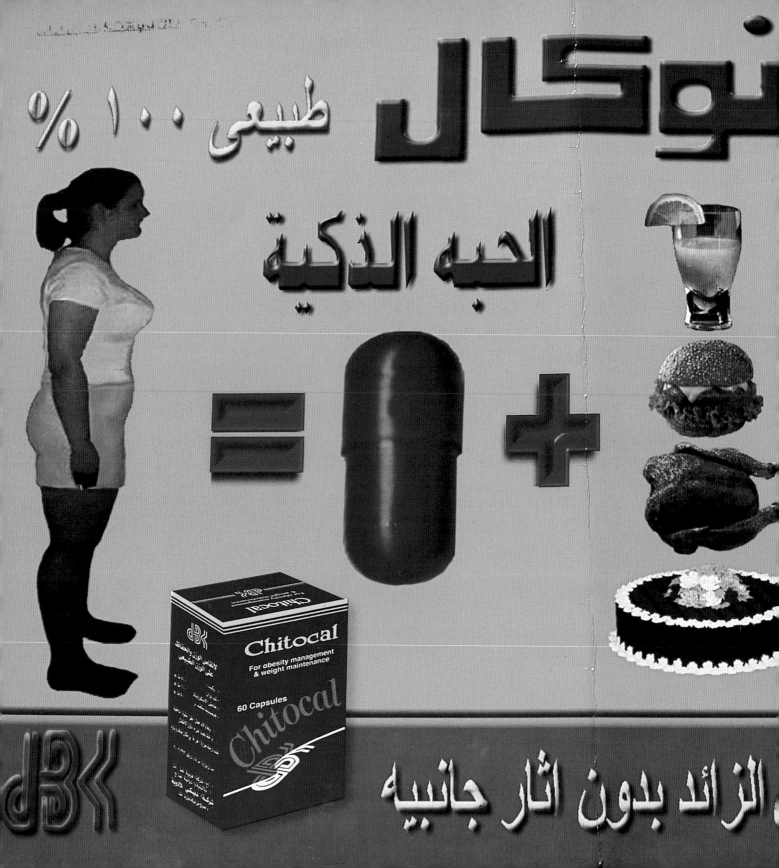

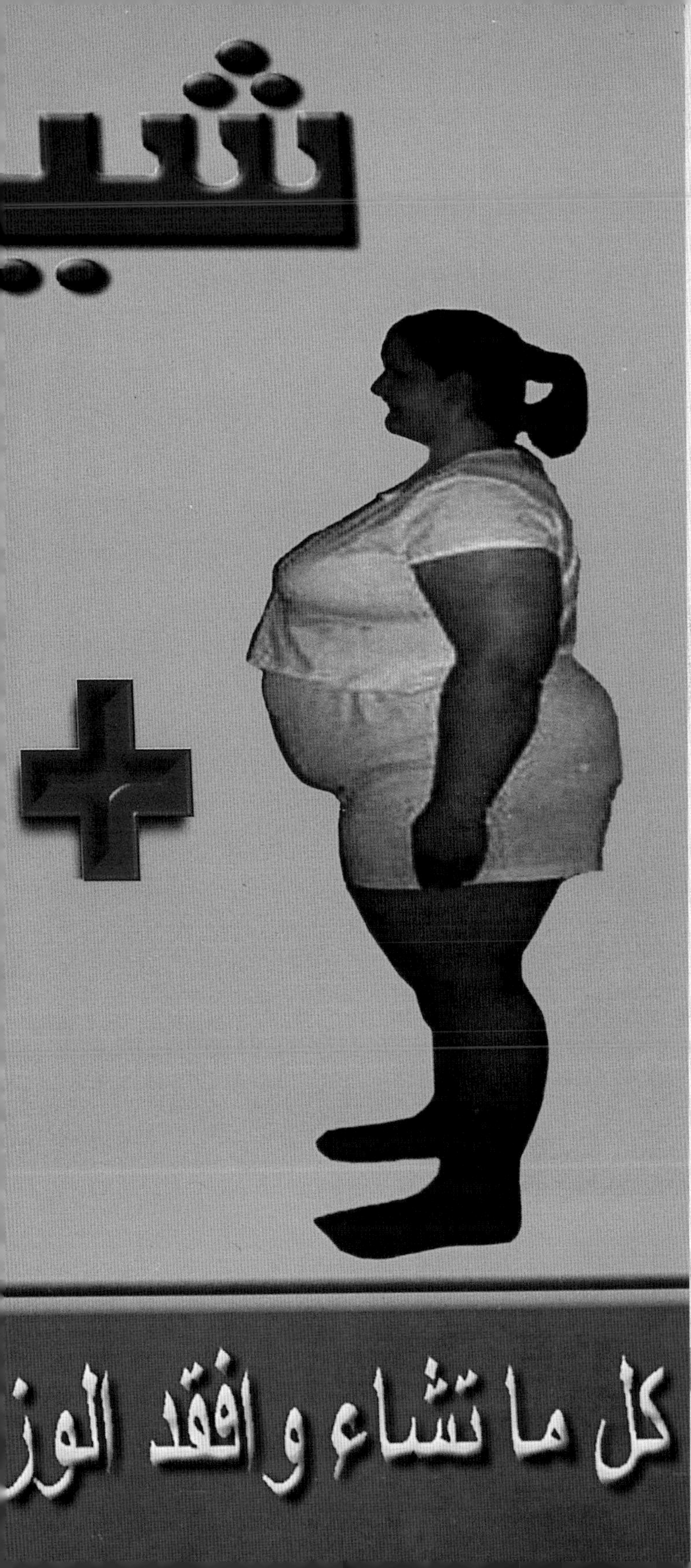

# EATING & DRINKING

'O ye who give cakes and ale to the shining ones, grant ye that my soul may be with you.'

*The Egyptian Book of the Dead*

PIZZA

**Opposite** An advertisement in a Cairo chemist's window makes powerful dieting claims, whichever way the equation is read.

كل ما تشاء وافقد الوز

75

Previous pages Restaurant signs in the Nubian city of Aswan.
Above and below The logos of American fast-food chains retain their familiarity despite rendering in Arabic script.
Below centre Posters urging a boycott of multinationals are ignored by most of the Egyptians that stand in line outside McDonald's each evening.

Below In the former city of Thebes, behind the 18th-dynasty pillars of Amenhotep's Luxor Temple, is a McDonald's restaurant with a permanent armed police guard.

Overleaf A neon Coca-Cola sign in Arabic is an evening landmark in Cairo's Midan Tahrir square.

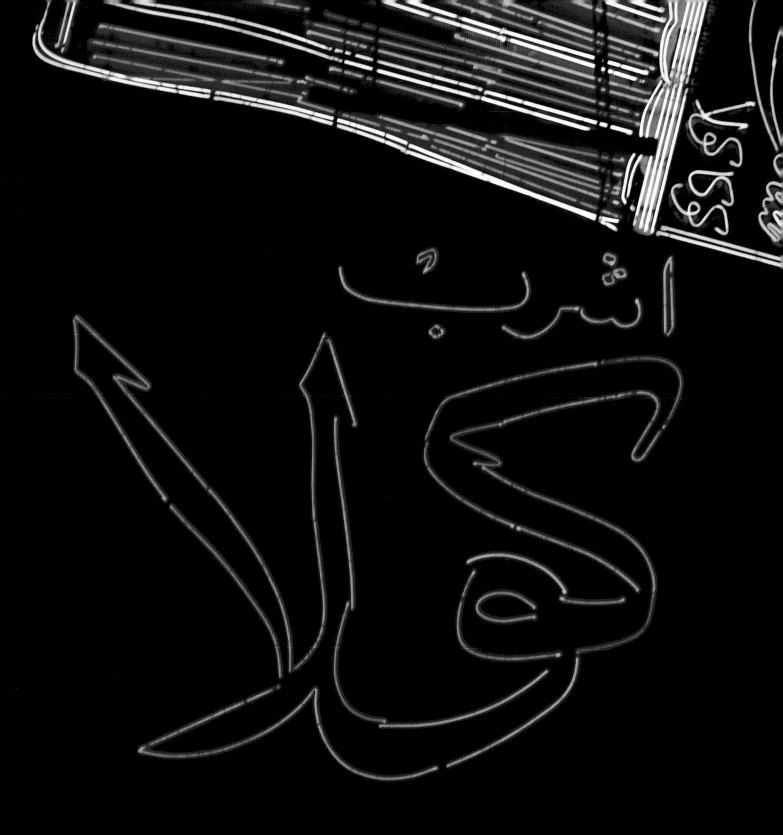

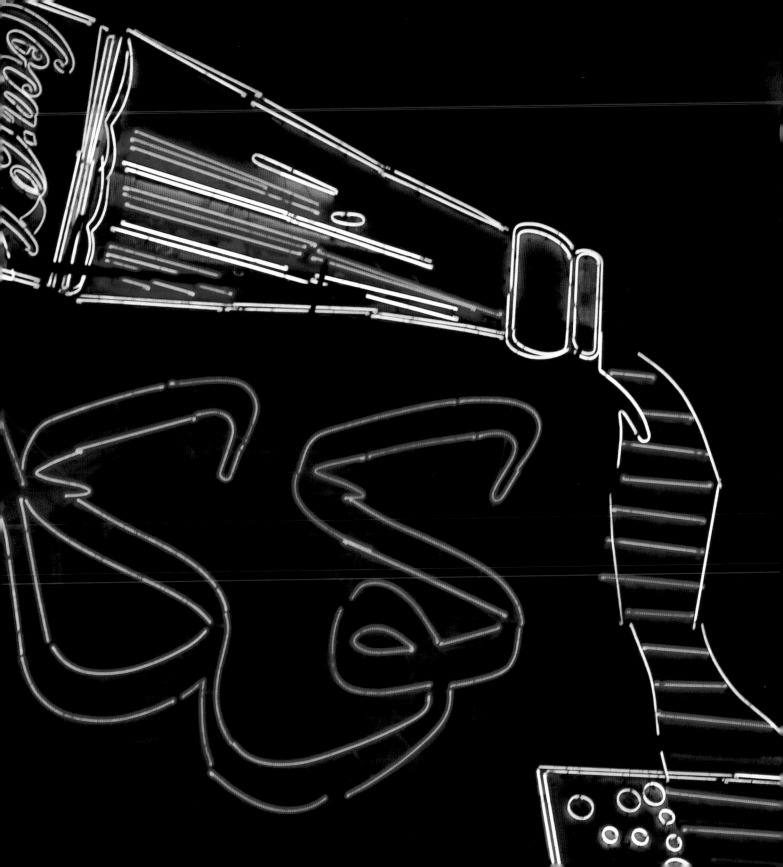

**Preceding pages**
**Page 82** Beer mats advertising Stella, so popular that the name has become the generic term for beer in Egypt.
**Page 83** A store in Luxor's souk with Coca-Cola advertising.

DATTES **ORIENT**

CE FRUIT DELICIEUX CONTIENT
UNE FORTE PROPORTION DE
SIROP NATUREL ET UNE
GRANDE PORTION DE VITAMINE

MARQUE DÉPOSÉE

Product packaging, store signs, and a market stall selling henna hair dyes.

**Overleaf** A collection of matchboxes, Cleopatra cigarettes and a souvenir lighter.

# ENTERTAINMENT

'...I will give you the best of the
land of Egypt and you can enjoy
the fat of the land.'

Pharaoh, Genesis 45:18

**Opposite** A cinema poster promoting an
Egyptian film, above a row of Western
movie posters in Cairo's Midan Tahrir.

Popular Egyptian cinema posters are fairly rigid in execution: actors in slapstick poses cover most genres.

# **S**ELF **A**DHESIVE
## EYEBROWS & MOUSTACHE

MADE IN CHINA

**Opposite and below** Masks and monsters – prizes, rides and decorative paintings in the amusement parks of Alexandria and Cairo.

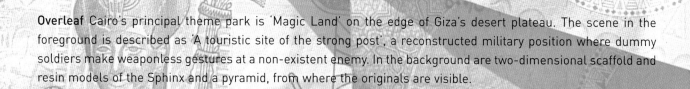

**Overleaf** Cairo's principal theme park is 'Magic Land' on the edge of Giza's desert plateau. The scene in the foreground is described as 'A touristic site of the strong post', a reconstructed military position where dummy soldiers make weaponless gestures at a non-existent enemy. In the background are two-dimensional scaffold and resin models of the Sphinx and a pyramid, from where the originals are visible.

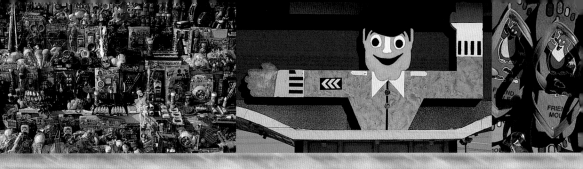

**Above** Images from fairgrounds and parks in Cairo.
**Below** Details from toy stall displays at Cairo fairgrounds.

# PAPYRUS

'And so the gods entered into their bodies, of every kind of wood, of every kind of stone, of every kind of clay, of every kind of thing which grows....'

*The Memphite Theology*

**Opposite** A modern interpretation of how the pyramids and sphinx of Giza might have looked in their heyday, on a painted papyrus souvenir. The writing paper of ancient Egypt is made from reeds and available on every street corner in major cities.

**Previous pages** Painted papyrus images of (left) Tutankhamun's golden death mask, discovered by English archeologist Howard Carter in 1922, and (right) the head of Queen Nefertiti, from a sculpture now in the Egyptian Museum, Berlin.

**Background** Detail of the temple of Queen Hatshepsut at Deir el-Bahri on the west bank at Luxor, 15th century BC.

**Opposite** Horoscope and zodiac signs have their origins in ancient Egypt, the birthplace of astronomy and astrology. Here the zodiac is represented in a reproduction tomb painting.

**Above** Modern papyrus interpretations of portraits of ancient Egyptian royalty use contrasting colour and lighting techniques.

**Overleaf** An ancient Egyptian tomb image of circumcision is popularly reproduced on papyrus, postcards and T-shirts for the amusement of friends and family back home.

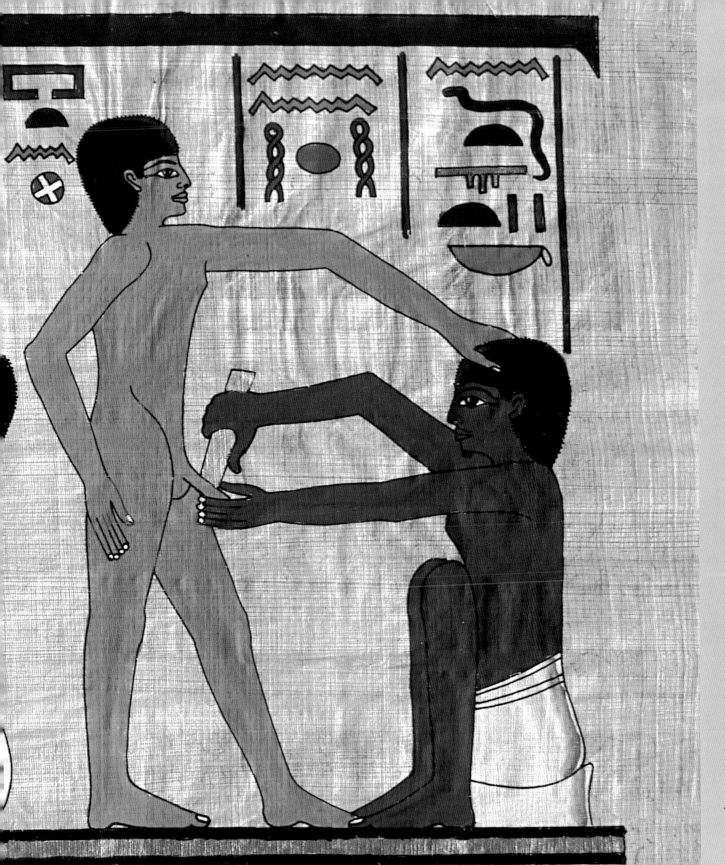

Reproductions of tomb paintings on darker, mature papyrus depict the falcon-headed god Horus with the pharaohs and fellow gods, all popular motifs in Egypt's tourist industry.

**Background** Detail of the entrance to the temple of Queen Hatshepsut (1490-68 BC) at Deir el-Bahri on the west bank of the Nile.

**Below left and opposite right** The ancient art of papyrus painting in the practical format of the modern souvenir: calendars that remind visitors of Egypt, its ancient culture and the transience of time.
**Centre** A papyrus painting features an ancient Egyptian barque with sea creatures beneath.

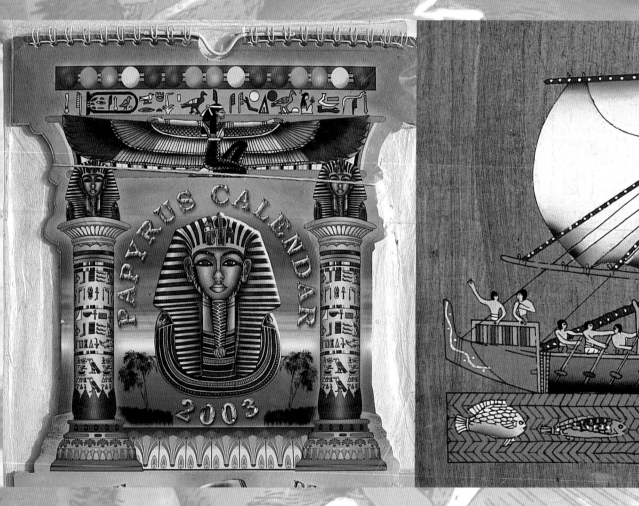

**Overleaf** A papyrus painting portrays the goddess Nut, who personified the sky.

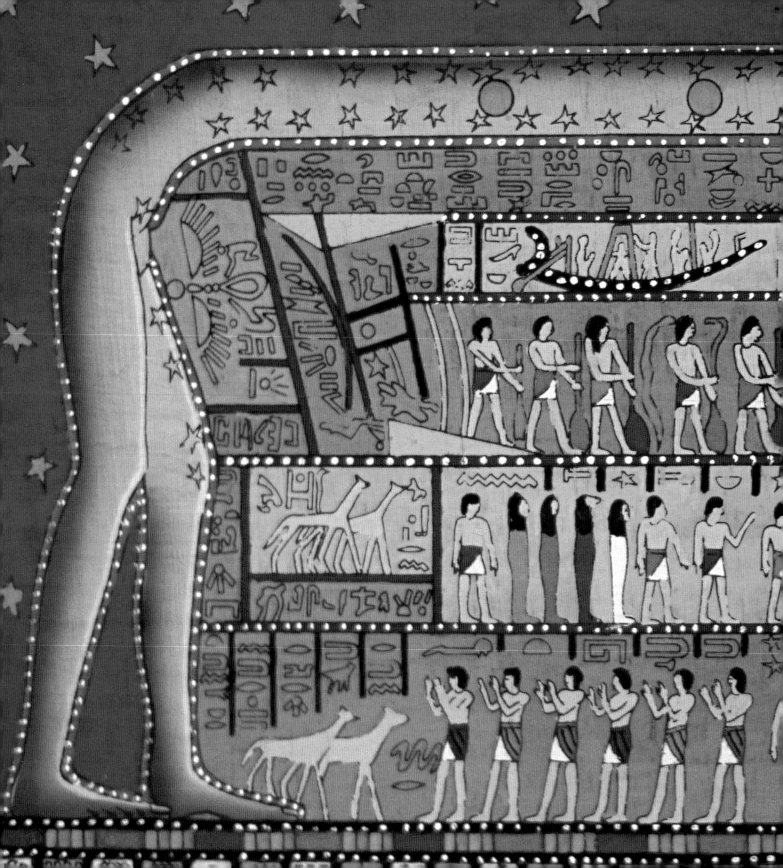

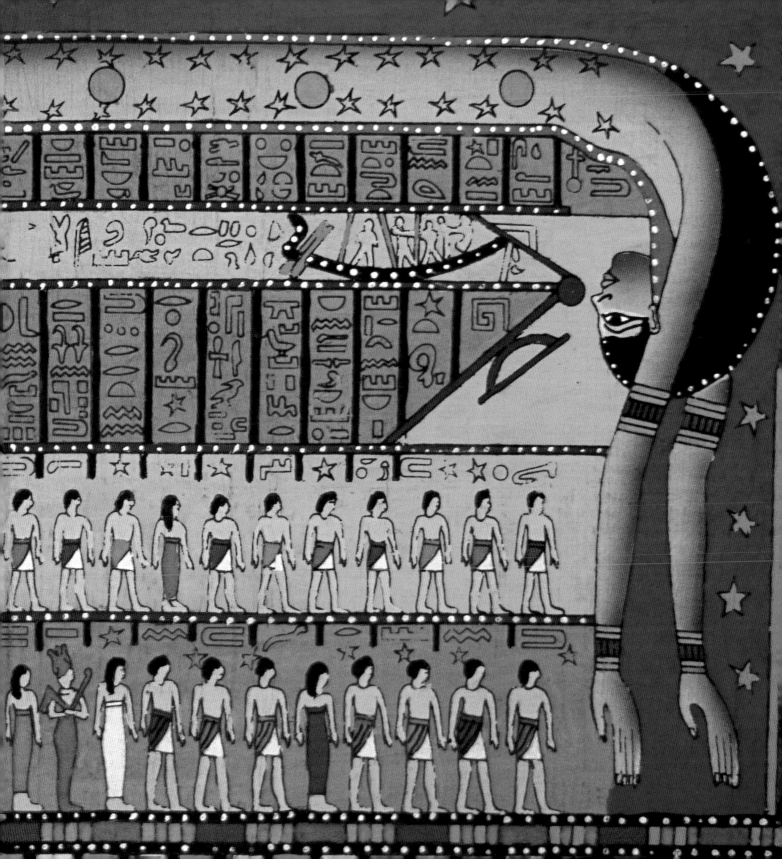

> **'What is past is dead.'**
>
> **Egyptian proverb**

Entry ticket to the tomb of Tutankhamun in Luxor's Valley of the Kings.